CRAFT ATTACK!

PRINTING CRAFTS

Annalees Lim

W

FRANKLIN WATTS

LONDON · SYDNEY

First published in 2014 by Franklin Watts

Copyright © 2014 Arcturus Publishing Limited

Franklin Watts
338 Euston Road
London NW1 3BH

Franklin Watts Australia
Level 17/207 Kent Street, Sydney NSW 2000

Produced by Arcturus Publishing Limited,
26/27 Bickels Yard, 151–153 Bermondsey Street, London SE1 3HA

Editors: Joe Harris and Sara Gerlings
Designer: Elaine Wilkinson
Cover design: Elaine Wilkinson
Photography: Simon Pask

A CIP catalogue record for this book is available from the British
Library.

Dewey Decimal Classification Number 745.4
ISBN 978 1 4451 2936 5

Printed in China

Franklin Watts is a division of Hachette Children's Books, an Hachette
UK company.

www.hachette.co.uk

SL003784UK
Supplier 03, Date 0114, Print Run 3035

CONTENTS

PERFECT PRINTING

When you hear the word 'printing', what do you think of? Do you imagine your desktop printer at home or a printing press churning out thousands of newspapers? Well, think again! Printing can be a lot more fun than that.

Stop the Press! Let's Get Printing

You don't need computers or machines to print. All that you really need are your own two hands and some simple craft materials. This book is full of easy, step-by-step printing projects. So grab some paints, follow the intructions and you will be making perfect prints every time!

Get the Look!

One of the best things about print-making is that you can print onto just about anything. Once you understand the basics, you'll be able to transform your clothes, books, stationery and even your room.

Keep It Clean

Getting messy is all in a day's work for a print-maker. Always lay newspaper or plastic over the surface you're working on and have a damp cloth close to hand for any small spills or splatters.

Rollers and Brushes

A good selection of paintbrushes and rollers will help you to create exciting prints. Synthetic brushes will work especially well. You will also need two different types of rollers – a fluffy roller to spread paint and a hard, rubber inking roller to spread inks and apply even pressure to create your prints.

Scissors and Craft Knives

Be careful when you use scissors. If you need to cut tougher materials such as plastic, ask an adult to help. <u>NEVER</u> use a craft knife without adult help.

Paints

For most printing, you can use acrylic or poster paints. When you are printing on clothes, bags or shoes, you will need to use fabric paint. Carefully follow the instructions on the fabric paint itself to make sure that it will be colour-fast. If the instructions say to use an iron, you should ask an adult to help.

PVA Glue

Sometimes called white glue, this works well for sticking together things like paper and wood.

Glue Stick

This is very easy to use and great for sticking together paper.

Fabric Glue

This is brilliant for sticking paper or card to fabric.

Craft Glue or Hobby Glue

This is useful if you need to stick on hard plastic things such as buttons or googly eyes.

APPLE PRINT CANVAS BAG

Printing with fruit and vegetables is easy and it looks great. This fruity canvas bag is perfect for making shopping trips. It saves on using plastic bags, so it's good for the environment!

1 Cut some apples in half. You may want to ask an adult to help.

2 Brush a thin layer of fabric paint onto a plastic chopping board.

3 Press the flat part of the apple onto the paint, making sure that the whole flat surface of the apple is covered.

4 Firmly press the apple onto the canvas bag. When you lift it off, you will reveal an apple-shaped print!

5 Repeat steps 3–4 until you have covered the whole bag, changing colours if you like. Leave to dry. Then check the instructions on your fabric paint. If the instructions say that you should use an iron to fix the paint, ask an adult to help you.

BLOCK PRINTED CARDS

Relief prints are usually made by cutting into wood. Here's how you can create the same effect with craft foam!

1 Draw shapes onto craft foam and cut them out with scissors. For a bee, you will need a large oval, two teardrop shapes, a triangle and a small circle. For flowers, you will need three large circles and eight small ones.

2 Cut each of the small circles in half. Cut the large oval into three parts, and snip into one part to give your bee an eye and a mouth.

3 Stick the shapes onto the wooden block using craft glue. Leave them to dry.

4 Paint or roller a thin layer of paint onto the block. Then press it onto the card.

5 Carefully lift the block to reveal your design. Repeat steps 3 and 4 if you would like to print more cards.

ONE-OFF PORTRAIT PRINT

Here is a project that makes only one final print. It can never be repeated, so it is unique! This type of printing is called a monoprint. A monoprint portrait makes a great gift.

1 Using a brush, paint a brightly coloured rectangle onto your plastic chopping board.

2 Now paint a frame around your rectangle in different colours.

3 Leave this for a couple of minutes so that it begins to dry, and then draw the outline of your portrait, using a cotton bud. Make sure that you press firmly!

4 Use the cotton bud to draw some patterns onto your painted frame.

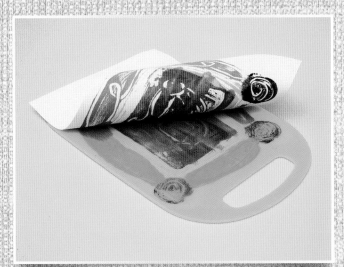

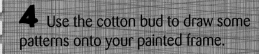

FUNKY PATTERN PRINTS

Here is a good way of printing repeating patterns. When you have finished making your print, you could frame it and hang it on the wall.

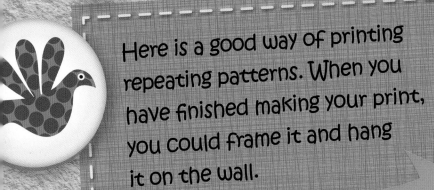

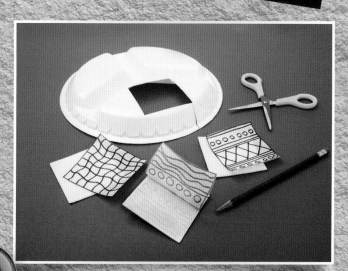

1 Draw some squares on a plain piece of paper using a black marker pen. Decorate each square with a different pattern. Cut out the squares with scissors.

2 Now cut some squares of the same size from your styrofoam plate. Place the paper squares on top of your styrofoam sqaures. Trace the lines using a blunt pencil. Push hard, to make a deep groove.

3 Use the foam roller to cover the styrofoam squares with a thin layer of paint. If you don't have a foam roller, you could use a normal paintbrush.

4 Starting in the top left-hand corner of your paper, place the styrofoam down and use the printing roller to apply firm and even pressure. If you don't have a printing roller, you could use a rolling pin wrapped in cling film.

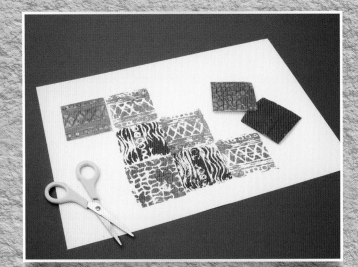

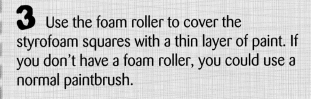

Remove the styrofoam to reveal your print. Repeat steps 4 and 5 again and again to make more prints on your paper. Leave your print to dry, then cut it out.

STENCIL ART PLANT POT

Because the stencils in this project are flexible, you can use them to print on curved surfaces! You will need an adult to help you with cutting out the stencils. Never use a craft knife without adult supervision.

1 Draw your design onto a piece of paper.

2 Trace the lines of your drawing onto tracing paper, but leave little spaces in the lines. Then trace the outline onto a separate piece of tracing paper, and colour it in.

3 Trace the spaced-line drawing and the outline drawing onto acetate paper. Ask an adult to cut out everything coloured black on the acetate sheets with a scalpel or craft knife.

4 Fix the stencil with the larger cut-out areas to the clay pot, using your masking tape.

5 Paint everything inside the template area blue and leave to dry.

CLAY PRINTING

You will need:
- Air-drying clay
- Clay tools
  (or ordinary cutlery)
- Rolling pin
- String
- Printing roller
- Foam roller
- Paint
- Sturdy paper

1 Roll out your clay so that you have a piece that is 1 cm (0.3 in) thick and smaller than your piece of paper.

2 Place your string on top of the clay in an interesting pattern. Press down to make an imprint before you remove it.

3 Use clay tools (or a knife and fork) to add more details in the clay.

4 Roll a thin layer of paint onto the clay.

5 Place a piece of paper on top and use either another roller or your hands to press it down.

6 Remove the paper to reveal your print.

When you have finished your prints, make a hole at the top of the clay slab before leaving it to dry. When the clay has hardened you can hang it up as a plaque!

ROLLER PRINT FOLDERS

Rolling pin prints make excellent repeat patterns. You never know quite what they will look like until you have started to roll! You can use this technique to personalise your school folders.

You will need

Cling film
Rolling pin
Paper
Self-adhesive craft foam sheets
Scissors
Blank non-glossy ring bind folder
Acrylic paint
Plastic chopping board
Sticky tape

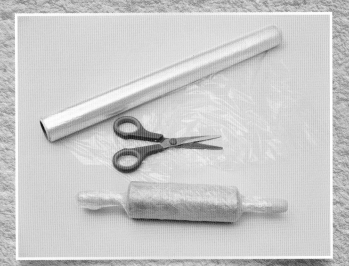

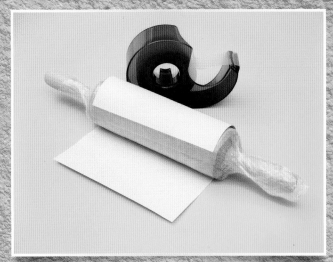

1 Cover the whole rolling pin with some cling film.

2 Cut out a piece of card that will fit around the rolling pin and fix into place using a piece of sticky tape.

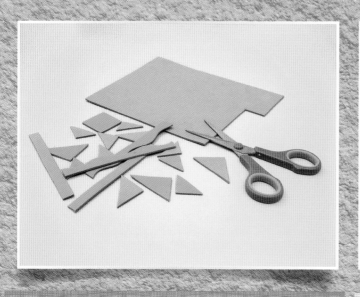

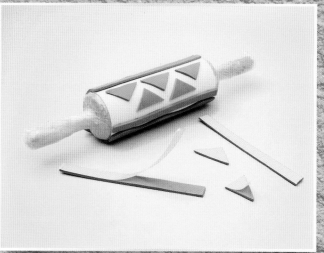

3 Cut out lots of shapes from your craft foam, using scissors. You will need enough shapes to cover nearly all of the rolling pin.

4 Peel off the backing from the craft foam and stick it onto the rolling pin. You will need to make sure that you space them evenly to make a print without big gaps.

5 Spread an even layer of paint onto the chopping board and roll the rolling pin through the paint.

CLING FILM WRAPPING PAPER

Cling film may be good for wrapping up food, but it's also great for craft projects. This cool wrapping paper will really make your gifts stand out from the rest!

You will need

Plastic chopping board
Cling film
Aluminium foil
Paper and scissors
Poster paint and silver paint
Paintbrushes

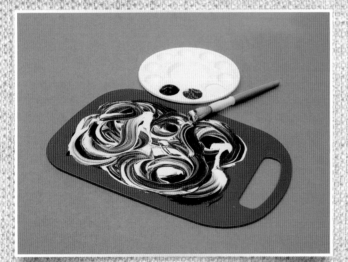

1 Spread three colours of paint onto your chopping board, swirling them together with your paintbrush to make a pattern.

2 Put a square of cling film onto the paint mixture and press it down.

3 Carefully lift the cling film and lower it onto your paper. You do not want it to be a flat print so it doesn't matter if it scrunches up. Lift off the cling film to reveal your pattern.

4 Repeat steps 2–3 until you have covered the whole piece of paper. Leave to dry.

5 For some added sparkle, coat the chopping board with silver paint. Scrunch up some aluminium foil and press it onto the silver paint. Then press it onto the paper.

BUTTON PRINT TRAINERS

Here is how you can make your old trainers look fresh and exciting! This type of printing uses found objects. If you don't want to use buttons or don't have any to hand, you can try using bottle tops instead.

1 Glue some buttons onto the top of bottle corks, using craft glue. Leave them to dry.

2 Use a paintbrush to paint a layer of fabric paint onto one of the button stamps.

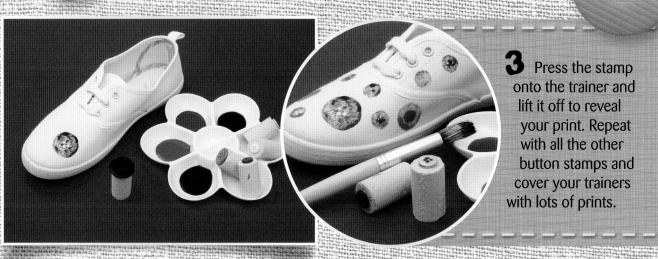

3 Press the stamp onto the trainer and lift it off to reveal your print. Repeat with all the other button stamps and cover your trainers with lots of prints.

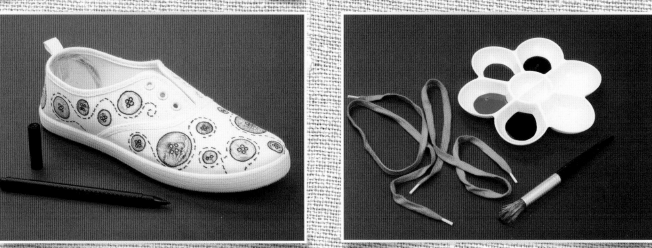

4 Add to your design using a black felt-tip pen.

5 Paint the laces in a bright colour and leave them to dry. Finally, check the instructions for your fabric paint. If you need to use an iron to fix the paint, ask an adult to help.

EASY SCREEN PRINTS

Screen printing is similar to stencil printing, except that the ink is pushed through a mesh using a tool called a squeegee. If you do not have a squeegee, try using a plastic card instead.

You will need

- Wooden frame (an old photo frame will work)
- Drawing pins
- Voile (fine netting)
- PVA glue
- Paint and paintbrush
- Plastic card
- Paper and pencil
- Black marker

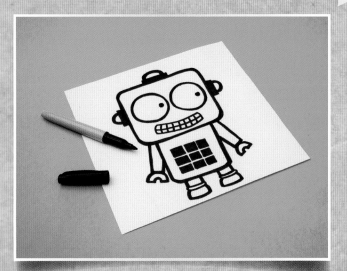

1 Draw a pattern or illustration onto a piece of paper, using bold, heavy lines.

2 Stretch some voile netting across a frame, and ask an adult to pin it in place.

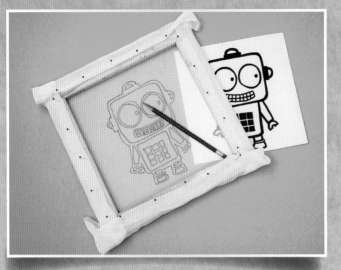

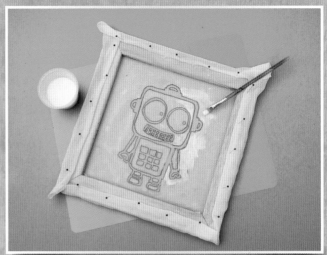

3 Trace around the outside of the black lines in your design onto the netting, using a fine pencil line.

4 First, protect your surface! Paint over the whole screen with PVA glue, except for the areas inside your pencil lines. Do the same to the other side. Leave it to dry.

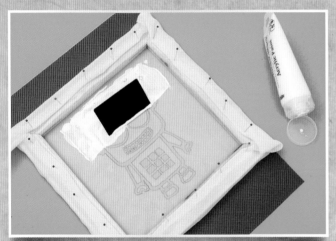

SPOTTY PAINTED MUGS

Teatime will never be dull again with this personalised mug. But beware, once you have a mug that looks this good, everyone will want to use it!

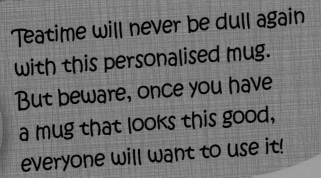

1 Measure around your mug, then measure the height and cut a piece of paper to the same size. Use this to draw your design onto.

2 Tape some carbon paper onto the mug, and then tape your design on top of that.

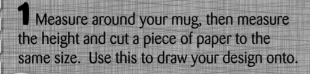

3 Trace over your design with a pencil, pressing hard. Then remove the papers from the mug to reveal a faint print.

4 Start to paint on the mug by dabbing on ceramic paint with a cotton bud.

5 Keep stippling (dotting) on the ceramic paint until you have finished your picture! Then you will need to follow the instructions on the label of your ceramic paint to make it set. Most ceramic paints will need to be baked in the oven.

WARNING!
If the instructions for the ceramic paint tell you to use the oven, ask an adult to help. Don't do this on your own!

BUBBLE PRINT T-SHIRT

Don't pop it, print it! Bubble wrap makes fun spotty prints. Your friends will be impressed when they see your bubble print t-shirt!

You will need
Bubble wrap
Scissors
Fabric paint
Black t-shirt
Piece of cardboard to stop the paint soaking through
Plastic chopping board
Paintbrush

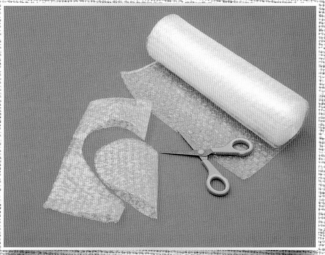

1 Fold a piece of bubble wrap in half and cut out a teardrop shape, as shown above. When you unfold it, it will make a heart.

2 Paint a thin layer of red paint onto the plastic chopping board.

3 Add some other colours of paint to the pallet, using a paintbrush.

4 Lay the outer part of the bubble wrap down in the paint. Press it down firmly.

5 Transfer the bubble wrap onto the t-shirt and press it down firmly. Lift the bubble wrap to reveal the print! Leave it to dry. Then repeat steps 3–5 with the heart shape and a different colour of paint. Finally, check the instructions for your fabric paint. If you need to use an iron to fix the paint, ask an adult to help.

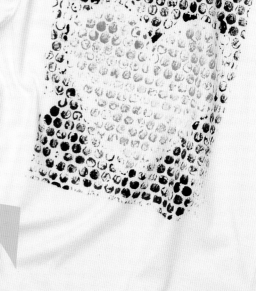

SANDPAPER PRINTING

You may think that sandpaper is only good for making things smooth... but think again! It's great for making one-off prints onto fabric too. We've used this technique to decorate a pencil case.

1 Cut a piece of sandpaper to the same shape as the pencil case. Draw a design on it, using coloured crayons.

2 Keep adding to your picture to fill the whole space. Make sure that you press down firmly, to create a thick layer of wax.

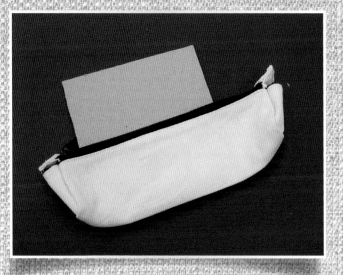

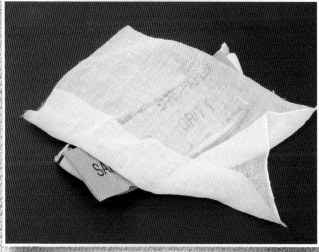

3 Place a piece of card underneath the fabric that you are going to transfer the pattern onto. We've placed it inside the pencil case.

4 Place your sandpaper onto your fabric with the pattern facing down. Cover it with a tea towel or piece of fabric.

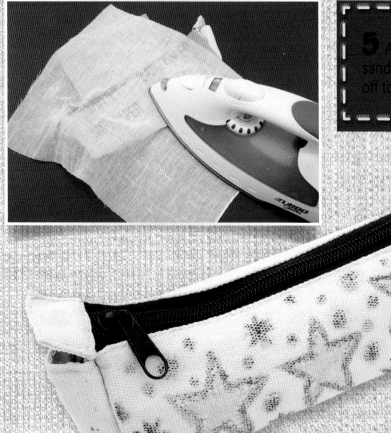

5 Ask an adult to iron on top of the sandpaper for two to three minutes. Then lift it off to reveal the pattern on your pencil case.

GLOSSARY

acetate A transparent sheet of plastic.

environment The world of nature.

relief printing A printing technique where raised shapes or letters are covered in ink, before being pressed onto a surface.

stencil printing A printing technique where ink or paint is pushed through a pattern that has been cut into a sheet of plastic, card or metal.

stippling A technique in drawing or painting where the artist makes a series of small dots or marks.

Ed Emberley's Complete Funprint Drawing Book by Ed Emberley (Little, Brown, 2005)

Stencil Art by Paula Hannigan (Klutz, 2007)

The Usborne Book of Art Skills by Fiona Watt (Usborne Publishing Ltd, 2008)

kids.nationalgeographic.co.uk/kids/activities/crafts/
Crafts inspired by nature.

spoonful.com/crafts
Crafts and activities for a range of ages.

www.firstpalette.com
A range of bright and colourful crafts for every occasion.

INDEX

SERIES CONTENTS

Jewellery Crafts

Make Your Own Jewellery • Pendant Necklace • Lucky Rabbit Earrings • Brilliant Bead Bracelet • Knotted Bracelet • Cool Collar Necklace • Fabric Flower Ring • Friends Forever Necklaces • Sew Easy Felt Brooch • Funky Toy Hair Clips • Jewelled Cuff • Puzzle Piece Hair Comb • Button Bag Charm • Jewellery Tree

Nature Crafts

Going Wild with Nature Crafts • Woodland Photo Frame • Painted Pebble Plant Pot • Butterfly Bunting • Sand Art • Shell Creature Fridge Magnets • Pressed Flower Coasters • Leafy Bird Mobile • Seed Mosaic • Japanese Blossom Tree • Pebble Zoo • Brilliant Bird Box • Pine Cone Field Mouse • Lavender Hand Warmers

Paper Crafts

Getting Crafty with Paper • Cube Puzzle • Pop-Up Painting • Paper Planets • Paper Pulp Monsters • Make Your Own Notebook • Secret Seashell Storage Box • 3-D Photo Art • Quilling Cards • Giant Crayons • Paper Globe Lampshade • Paper Cup Disco Ball • Envelopes and Notepaper • Paper Bouquet

Printing Crafts

Perfect Printing • Apple Print Canvas Bag • Block Printed Cards • One-Off Portrait Print • Funky Pattern Prints • Stencil Art Plant Pot • Clay Printing • Roller Print Folders • Cling Film Wrapping Paper • Button Print Trainers • Easy Screen Prints • Spotty Painted Mugs • Bubble Print T-Shirt • Sandpaper Printing

Recycling Crafts

Crafty Recycling • Jam Jar Lanterns • Bottle Tops in Bloom • Funny Face Vase • Stackable Rocket Boxes • Beach Hut Pen Pots • Bedroom Pinboard • Water Bottle Bracelets • Scrap Paper Daisy Chain • Peacock Bookends • Sunny Days Clock • Starry Sky Mail Mobile • CD Case Photo Frame • Plastic Bag Weaving

Textile Crafts

Terrific Textiles • Cute Sock Owls • Rock Star Rag Doll • Toadstool Doorstop • Funky Felt Friend • Cocoa Cosy • Totally Brilliant Tote • Awesome Accessories • Jean Genius Desk Mascot • Secret Diary Cover • Mini Bag Organizer • Cupcake Pincushion • Knitted Phone Case